MUSEUM OF ART

MASTERPIECES

RUTH THOMSON

RUNNING PRESS
PHILADELPHIA · LONDON

A QUARTO CHILDREN'S BOOK

Copyright 2001 Quarto Children's Books Ltd

9 8 7 6 5 4 3 2 1
Digit on the right indicates the number of this
printing.

Library of Congress Cataloging-in-Publication
Number 2001087049

ISBN 0-7624-1067-1

This book was designed and produced by
Quarto Children's Books Ltd
The Fitzpatrick Building
188–194 York Way
London N7 9QP

PUBLISHERS Robert Morley / Aline Littlejohn
EDITOR Samantha Sweeney
ART DIRECTOR Terry Woodley
DESIGNER Caroline Grimshaw

Manufactured in China

This kit may be ordered by mail from the publisher.
Please include $2.50 for postage and handling.
But try your bookstore first!

Running Press Book Publishers
125 South Twenty-second Street
Philadelphia, Pennsylvania 19103-4399

Visit us on the web!
www.runningpress.com

Contents

What's in Your Museum of Art?

Your museum kit is full of amazing activities to help you discover more about the world of art. As you read the book, you'll find out what influenced artists to paint pictures, and how they painted them.
The activities in your kit and throughout the book will let you see for yourself the processes involved in showing and restoring paintings today. Words relating to art terms and techniques, which may be new to you, are underlined, and explained in the glossary at the back of the book.

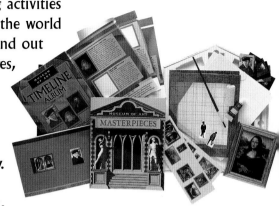

▲ Inside your kit, you'll find everything you need to complete the activities explained on this page.

▲ Use the tools provided to clean and restore the *Mona Lisa*.

Framed mini masterpiece

Paintings many centuries old sometimes need to be carefully restored to show their original colors. Over many years, paintings can become damaged by sunlight, or simply get very dirty. Use the equipment provided to restore the masterpiece in your kit.
Dampen the cleaning fabric, and gently wipe over the picture to remove surface dirt. Repeat the process if necessary. Then, touch up any damaged areas by carefully applying dabs of paint with the paintbrush. When your masterpiece is restored to its former glory, hang it up for everyone to admire!

▲ Complete your timeline album by placing the artist portraits in the correct spaces.

Mini art gallery and stickers

Fold the cardboard model out of your kit, and become the curator of your very own gallery! Consider carefully how many paintings you wish to exhibit, and how you will arrange each one. The stickers are faithful reproductions of a selection of paintings featured in your book. They are different shapes and sizes; some are landscape, some portrait. On the next page you will find details about how paintings used to be displayed, and how galleries arrange them to best effect now.

Timeline album

This concertina timeline album helps you to find out about the lives of famous artists—from Cimabue, a mosaicist and painter of the thirteenth century, to Impressionists, Renoir and Degas, in the nineteenth century. Add the artist portraits in the spaces provided, and learn about art movements, and techniques through the ages.

▲ A model art gallery folds out of your kit. Use the artwork stickers to complete your mini gallery.

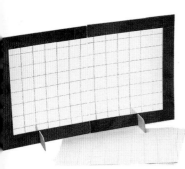

◄ Use the grid to practice drawing in proportion.

Drawing grid

Use the plastic grid to help you draw to scale, just as famous artists like Leonardo da Vinci did in the 15th century. Place the grid in front of you, and draw the view you see through it.

What Is an Art Museum?

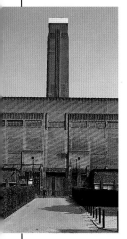

An art museum displays a collection of original paintings, and sometimes also sculptures, drawings, photographs and prints. Many of the paintings are hundreds of years old. They are never displayed haphazardly. Some museums group pictures according to where they were painted, either by country or by continent. Other museums group them century by century. Sometimes pictures painted at the same time and in the same country are hung together. Alternatively, pictures may be hung according to their theme, such as landscapes or portraits, or separate rooms are given over to a collection of paintings by particular artists. The person who decides how paintings will be displayed is called a curator.

The first art museums

Very few pictures made before the twentieth century were painted to be seen in a museum. In fact, art museums did not exist before the eighteenth century. Some major European art museums were once royal palaces, with huge collections amassed by powerful rulers, and were not open to the public.

The Louvre, in Paris, was once a royal palace. It became the first national public art museum in the world when it was seized from the king after the French Revolution.

From the outside . . .

In the nineteenth century, many public art museums were built in Europe and the U.S., so that anyone could come and enjoy great works of art. Some, including the National Gallery of Art, Washington D.C., look like grand palaces, and have entrances that resemble temples in ancient Greece or Rome.

The Louvre, Paris, France

More recently, some immense industrial buildings have been converted into art museums. The Tate Modern in London, England (pictured far left), was once used as a power station.

In the last 20 years, some cities have built new art museums. The buildings, designed by world-famous architects, are often unusual and exciting. Even the buildings themselves have become major tourists sights. The Guggenheim in Bilbao, Spain (pictured above), is an example.

. . . looking in

The inside of an art museum is often as splendid as the outside. The old paintings it displays once belonged in other buildings such as churches and monasteries, town halls, palaces, or people's homes. The galleries are deliberately decorated in a way that reflects the original setting of the pictures (although light comes in from the ceiling, instead of through windows, to help preserve the paintings from the sun). Large, imposing pictures, designed to be seen from a distance, are often hung at the end wall of a gallery or in the biggest galleries. Small pictures, which originally hung in ordinary people's homes, are arranged in smaller, more intimate spaces.

In the past, pictures were crowded from floor to ceiling, in no specific order. Some paintings were even cut down to fit into a particular room! Nowadays pictures are mostly hung at eye level with enough space between them so that you can concentrate on one at a time.

The Salle Rouge, Louvre, Paris, France.

The Tour Starts Here!

Looking at paintings

Come and visit the virtual museum in this book, to view a collection of pictures painted between the 1200s and 1800s by many celebrated European and American artists. In this virtual museum, the pictures have been arranged by theme, so you can discover why and how artists, living in different places and painting hundreds of years apart, have depicted particular subjects.

Remember, however, that all these pictures are only reproductions. They can't and don't have the presence of the original paintings—you won't be able to get the full impact of their size, whether big or small, the quality of their paint texture, whether smooth or raised, or the trueness of their colors, whether glowing or sombre. If you get the chance to look at some real paintings in an art museum, seize it!

To make the most of a museum visit, follow these useful tips:

● Don't try to see too much, and don't stay too long—otherwise you will get "museumitis!"

● Browse around until one picture catches your eye, and then stop to take a really long look at it. View it from afar to notice what seems to be the most important part of it, and what impact it has on you. Come nearer to have a close look at the way the artist has painted it, and check out small details.

● Since most pictures were never designed to be in a museum, ask yourself some questions. First think about where a picture might originally have hung. Would it have been in a church, a public building, or someone's home? Who might have wanted it, and why? Does it celebrate an event, or tell a story? Was it a love token, a souvenir of a visit, or did it inspire prayer?

● Hunt for clues that will tell you more about the picture. The more questions you ask, and the more you look, the more you will see.

Gallerie des Batailles, Chateau de Versailles, France

Questions to ask about a portrait

✔ Who might have asked for this portrait to be made?
✔ Where do you think it might originally have hung?
✔ How much of the picture does the figure take up?
✔ How would you describe the man's character?
✔ What does his expression tell you? Is he proud, dreamy, cruel or amused?
✔ What impression does he make on you? Would you like him?
✔ What is his pose like—tense or relaxed?
✔ What sort of clothes is he wearing? Do they tell you more about him?
✔ Is he looking at you? If so, is it eye-to-eye, or is he looking down at you?
✔ What do the background details tell you about his way of life, his job and his interests?
✔ Is this portrait realistic, or do you think the artist tried to flatter the sitter?
✔ Do you think the sitter was pleased with his portrait?

Henry VIII by Hans Holbein the Younger

A Storm in the Rocky Mountains by Albert Bierstadt

Questions to ask about a landscape

✔ Why might the artist have painted this landscape and for whom?
✔ Does it feel real or imaginary?
✔ What is the viewpoint—has the picture been painted as if you were on top of a hill, walking along a path or standing on a grassy plain?
✔ How has the artist suggested space and distance? How do the colors change from the foreground to the background? Is there a route that leads your eye through the picture?
✔ Is this a peaceful or dramatic scene?
✔ What time of day might it be?
✔ What time of year might it be?
✔ If you could walk into this picture, what would you hear and smell?
✔ What did the artist feel?
✔ How does this landscape make you feel—happy or sad, frightened or exhilarated?

Angels and Gold

The oldest European pictures in art galleries date back about 700 years.

Virtually all of them were originally made for Christian churches. Influential families and important church officials commissioned (ordered and paid for) holy pictures for their private chapels, or to stand above the main altar where the priest said mass. These were called <u>altarpieces</u>, and usually showed a scene in the life of Jesus Christ or his mother, the Virgin Mary. They were painted with the most precious materials of the time.

The Madonna

This huge painting, over twice the height of a tall person, was commissioned as an altarpiece for a church in Florence. In the candlelight of a dim church, all the gold would have sparkled and glinted in just the way the people in the Middle Ages thought that heaven glowed. The eight angels carry the Madonna (the Virgin Mary) on a golden throne, to become Queen of Heaven. She is holding her son, baby Jesus.

The four men in the arches are prophets, who foretold the coming of Jesus long before his birth.

▶ **Cimabue (Cenni di Peppi)**
Madonna and Child Enthroned with Eight Angels, c.1280
<u>Tempera</u> on wood
151 x 88 in.
Uffizi Gallery, Florence, Italy

SPOTLIGHT

Altarpieces were painted on wooden panels, coated first with a smooth, white, chalky substance called gesso. The background was pure gold leaf—wafer-thin sheets made from beaten gold coins. The Madonna's blue dress was painted with ultramarine, a <u>pigment</u> far more expensive than gold. It was made from lapis lazuli, a rare mineral found only in distant Afghanistan.

LOOK CLOSER . . .

At the time Cimabue worked, no one could agree whether angels were male or female. He has carefully painted them so they look neither one nor the other, all dressed in long robes with multicolored wings.

Holy people were always shown with a golden disk, a halo, behind their heads. The halos were punched with patterns to catch the candlelight.

Mary points at Jesus to show his importance. Jesus holds up his hand in a gesture of blessing.

Painted Prayers

One popular theme of religious paintings, especially in Italy, was the biblical story of the Annunciation. This is when the Archangel Gabriel, God's chief messenger, announced to the Virgin Mary that God had chosen her to be the mother of Jesus.

Fra Angelico has depicted the moment just after the angel's announcement. Gabriel is shown on bended knee, with his head bowed to Mary. Mary sits on her stool, turned slightly toward us, but with her eyes cast down. Her meek expression shows that she has accepted God's will.

Fra Angelico was a very pious and devout painter, who wanted to reflect the bliss and glory of God in his art. He painted this graceful and peaceful picture for monks to contemplate as they prayed and meditated.

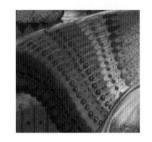

Gabriel's huge magnificent wings are his most eye-catching feature. The feathers are painted in an array of glowing colors.

A high fence separates Mary's flower garden from the wild countryside beyond. An enclosed garden, often seen in Annunciation paintings, symbolizes Mary's purity. ⎯⎯⎯

LOOK CLOSER . . .

Although Fra Angelico has invented an imaginary world, this picture includes all sorts of details he would have seen in real life. The decorated columns were drawn from ancient Roman ones, the trees were based on those that grew in northern Italy, and the artist probably copied the shape of the angel's wings from birds' wings.

Mary is not in <u>scale</u> with the building. If she stood up, she would bump her head on the ceiling!

This painting is one of about fifty <u>frescos</u> that Fra Angelico painted on the walls of the cloisters, chapter house, and cells (tiny rooms) of his fellow friars at the San Marco Monastery in Florence, Italy. A <u>fresco</u> is a wall painting made by mixing powdered colored pigments with water and applying them to a wet plaster wall. As the plaster dries, the colors become part of the wall, so they never flake off.

The crossed hands of both Mary and the Angel Gabriel are a sign of humility. Mary crosses her hands to show that she accepts what God has asked her to do. Gabriel kneels and humbly crosses his hands before Mary.

◄ **Fra Angelico (Giovanni da Fiesole)**
The Annunciation,
C.1438–1445
Fresco
40 x 28 in.
San Marco Museum, Florence, Italy

The Christmas Story

Events in the Christmas story were also popular themes for altarpieces or for small paintings which wealthy people used at home for private prayers. These showed *The Adoration of the Shepherds* or, more commonly, *The Adoration of the Magi* (the Three Wise Men). Compare how differently these two paintings depict these well-known Nativity events.

Two other shepherds shield their eyes from the bright light of the angel, who has come to give them the news about the birth of Jesus.

In *The Adoration of the Shepherds*, the stable feels very cramped and crowded with so many faces peering at the new-born baby Jesus. Mary, with her halo of bright rays, stands aloof in the center, gazing peacefully down at her child. Joseph, the angels, and the two shepherds bend their heads respectfully toward the infant in the manger, with their hands raised in worship. The large heads of an ox and a donkey loom over Joseph's shoulder, as if they are trying to see what is happening.

LOOK CLOSER . . .

The shepherds and Joseph have ruddy, lined faces, gnarled hands, and unkempt hair. Notice how real these men look compared to Mary, who has flawless white skin, unusually long fingers, and neat, flowing, golden locks, to emphasize her perfection.

Wide-eyed, baby Jesus faces out to the viewer, rather than looking at anyone in the stable. When someone kneeled to pray in front of this picture, he or she would have felt included in the scene.

▲ **Hugo van der Goes**
The Adoration of the Shepherds, c.1480
Tempera on panel
156 x 168 in.
Wilton House, Wiltshire, U.K.

‹ Hugo van der Goes
The Adoration of the Magi,
C. 1470
Oil on canvas
36.5 x 40.5 in.
The Hermitage,
St. Petersburg, Russia

This Wise Man holds a pot of frankincense— a symbol of homage to God.

This Wise Man has a jar of myrrh, an ointment used to embalm the dead.

The eldest Wise Man has brought gold— a symbol both of royalty and purity.

The Adoration of the Magi is much grander and shows several events at once. Two angels hold up a richly brocaded cloth behind Mary, which makes it seem as if she is sitting on a throne in this otherwise simple setting. The Three Wise Men lean forward to kneel before Christ, the new king, and offer him their gifts. Behind them, a long line of people jostle eagerly for a glimpse. Meanwhile, the Magi's servants can be seen relaxing on a nearby hillside, and a shepherd is startled at the appearance of an angel on another hill. Two more shepherds gaze at the Magi's arrival from above.

SPOTLIGHT

There was a tradition for painters to depict each of the Wise Men with very different characteristics as symbols of the various peoples of the world. One Wise Man is usually shown as a young man, another as a mature adult, the third as an old man, and each has different colored skin. They all wear richly decorated clothes, often trimmed with fur and jewels, sometimes reflecting the fashions of the time.

Famous People

Before the invention of cameras, <u>portraits</u> were the only way of recording what people looked like. Many artists made a successful living from painting portraits of wealthy and important people, who wanted a lasting reminder of themselves. Some portraits focus closely on a person's face or character, whereas others include

details that give a strong message about a person's status, achievements, or interests. But sometimes portraits lied! They showed people to be far more beautiful, heroic, or powerful than they really were.

Face to Face

Do you think this couple saw eye to eye? Federigo da Montefeltro, Duke of Urbino, a soldier and scholar, commissioned these portraits of himself and his wife Battista after her tragic death. It is possible that Battista's profile was copied from a mask made of her face after she died. Perhaps he wanted to take this reminder of her with him on his travels.

LOOK CLOSER . . .

Compare these two faces in detail. With her flawless, pale, porcelain skin and her tightly bound hair, Battista looks ageless, as though she has been frozen in time. Federigo, on the other hand, has been painted more realistically, with wrinkled eyes and skin, a double chin, and moles on his cheek.

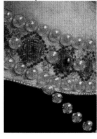

Through careful observation of light and shadow, Piero has made Battista's pearls and jewels sparkle very convincingly.

‹ Piero della Francesca
Federigo da Montefeltro and his wife Battista Sforza,
1472, tempera on wood, 18.5 x 13 in. each
Uffizi Gallery, Florence, Italy

Federigo's nose is this unusual shape, because it was shattered during the joust in which his eye was damaged. Piero makes a distinguishing feature of the nose, to help portray a true likeness of the duke—warts and all!

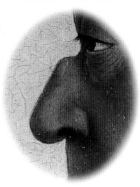

This landscape view is not of a real place. The panorama of plains and hills, stretching into the misty distance, probably suggests the immense expanse of the lands the duke ruled.

SPOTLIGHT

The Duke of Urbino was one of the most powerful and successful city rulers of Italy. These men wanted to impress people with their wealth and learning. They built elegant and expensive palaces, decorating them with murals and pictures, and filling them with books, sculptures, and precious gold and silver objects. They summoned the best artists of the day who, sometimes, worked at their courts for years at a time.

Flat-profile portraits, like these, were common at the time, but this left-hand-side view of Federigo also deliberately hides his scarred right eye. Federigo had unwisely left his helmet visor open during a joust, and was injured by his opponent's lance.

Piero was the first Italian artist to use landscape as a background for a portrait. It helps to make the portraits of these two intelligent, dignified people more imposing.

Kings and Queens

Kings and queens wanted their portraits to be as impressive as possible, so that everybody who saw them would be reminded of royal power.

The colossal body of Henry VIII, bulked out even further by his fine clothes, almost completely fills this full-length portrait. Far larger than life-size, Henry's portrait shows off the king's immense and alive physical presence. Standing ramrod straight, feet solidly apart, hand on hip, his imposing power is clear. The richness of his bejeweled clothes and the gorgeous drapes and carpet add to the feeling of grandeur.

▲ **Hans Holbein the Younger**
Henry VIII, c.1537
<u>Oil</u> on wood, dimensions 87 x 59 in.
Belvoir Castle, Leicestershire, U.K.

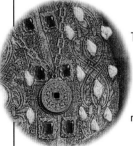

The colors and textures of Henry's clothes and jewels are painted in precise detail to give a feeling of fashionable magnificence.

Eastern carpets, like this, were a hugely expensive luxury in Henry VIII's time. They were often included in portraits as a sign of the sitter's great wealth.

LOOK CLOSER . . .
Compare the gaze of the two monarchs. Henry stares directly out toward the viewer, with an expression of stern authority. Elizabeth, on the other hand, gazes beyond the viewer, making her seem remote and unreachable.

Elizabeth I wanted her portraits to inspire awe. She used only the very best portrait artists and gave them strict instructions on how they should portray her. If she wasn't happy with a portrait, it was destroyed! Once she had approved a particular portrait, other painters were allowed to make faithful copies. Hundreds of copies were made for nobles to hang in their grand houses, as a sign of their support for the queen.

Elizabeth was about 41 years old at the time of this painting, but the white makeup she wore to cover her smallpox scars makes her look ageless. She is dressed in elaborate clothes, made of the finest materials, and bedecked with precious jewels, which she asked Hilliard to paint extra large to emphasize her wealth and royal status.

ACTIVITY

Use the practice paper in your kit to draw the portrait of a king (or queen). Think about the pose, expression and clothes, to make your picture as imposing as possible. Check that your picture is accurate and in proportion by using the grid provided in the kit.

▾ Nicholas Hilliard
Elizabeth I (The Pelican Portrait)
1574
Oil on wood, 31 x 24 in.
Walker Art Gallery, Liverpool, U.K.

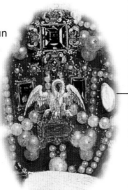

The Pelican brooch shows a mother pelican pecking her breast, so that she can feed her own blood to her hungry chicks. She may die but her children will live. Elizabeth saw herself like a mother pelican, ready to die for her children, the people of England.

Look Alive!

Gaze at Mona Lisa. Can you see how she seems to gaze right back at you, and her lopsided expression appears to move slightly, just like a living, moving person? Is she smiling with joy, sadness, scorn, or is she, as someone has suggested, grimacing with toothache? No one will ever know, but Mona Lisa's lifelike presence is what makes her portrait so renowned.

In addition to being the most famous painting in the world, protected in the Louvre Museum in Paris by thick, bulletproof glass, this picture is also one of the most mysterious. No one knows for certain who Mona Lisa was. She may have been the young wife of a wealthy Florentine nobleman, Francesco dal Giocondo, or she may have been Leonardo's image of the ideal woman. Nor does anyone know how long it took Leonardo to paint this picture. Some people think it took several years. It is known, however, that he took *Mona Lisa* with him when he went to live in France in 1516, and that he kept it until he died.

SPOTLIGHT

Mona Lisa's expression appears to flicker, because Leonardo deliberately blurred the corners of her eyes and mouth, so that they merge into the shadows. Leonardo invented this soft, smoky effect. It is known as *sfumato*. To achieve the gradual effect from dark to light, he painted many fine layers of transparent glaze between the layers of oil paint, so that light was reflected through them.

LOOK CLOSER . . .

The two imaginary landscapes on either side of Mona Lisa's head could not connect. The horizon line of the jagged peaks on the right is higher than the one on the left. Focus on one landscape and then the other and notice how the look of Mona Lisa changes.

No one is certain why Mona Lisa has no eyebrows. It may be because it was the fashion for ladies to pluck their eyebrows. Perhaps Leonardo did include eyebrows, but they were accidently wiped off when the painting was first restored or cleaned. Notice how carefully you have to remove the dirt from the mini masterpiece in your pack, to prevent damaging the painting.

▸ **Leonardo da Vinci**
Mona Lisa (La Gioconda)
C.1503–1506
Oil on panel, 30 x 21 in.
Louvre Museum, Paris, France

The strange, wild background with its bare, craggy mountains shrouded in hazy shadows looks very inhospitable. Leonardo has, however, included a narrow, winding path and a three-arched bridge as signs of human life.

Compare how sharply the folds of the sleeves have been painted compared with the rest of her clothes. Some experts believe that Leonardo changed his style during the time he took to do this painting.

A Leader on Horseback

Charles V, the Holy Roman Emperor, was the most important leader of his era. He ruled more of Europe than anyone had for over a thousand years. Titian's painting of him astride a horse was a new way of painting an important ruler. It was inspired by ancient Roman statues of their leaders on horseback.

Dressed in shining armor, firmly gripping his spear and looking resolutely ahead, Charles is shown riding home alone from a victorious battle, in which he had personally led his troops. Calm, and proudly in charge of his huge black, restless steed, Charles looks every inch a powerful and successful leader. Many other painters later copied this majestic horseback pose for their portraits of kings.

SPOTLIGHT

Notice how Titian uses color. The emperor's brightly glinting armor and pale face contrast strongly with his black horse and the dark woods behind him. The horse's head is outlined clearly against the glowing sky, and its front hooves stand out against the paler background.

The emperor is wearing richly decorated armor, but this was only for show. It would not have protected him from guns, which had been invented by this time.

LOOK CLOSER . . .

Titian deliberately painted the picture from a low <u>viewpoint</u>, to emphasize Charles V's dominating and powerful position. Because the emperor is seated so high up, viewers would have had to stand at a distance and look up at him. This would have made them feel small by comparison. Think about where you would place this painting if you were hanging it in the mini gallery in your pack.

The horse's red plume matches the emperor's. This would have helped the emperor's troops spot him from a distance.

Titian has set the emperor against wooded countryside with a hill in the distance. This was not the real landscape of the battle. Along with the reddening evening sky, the background helps create a calm, warm mood for this painting.

‹ **Titian**
(Tiziano Vecellio)
Emperor Charles V at Mühlberg, 1548
Oil on canvas
131 x 110 in.
Prado, Madrid, Spain

Searching for Clues

Sometimes the details in the background of a portrait may influence what you think about a person. Both these portraits are of famous soldiers who became leaders of their countries, but they convey very different images of leadership.

This full-length portrait celebrates the victory of the Americans, led by George Washington, over the British at the Battle of Princeton. Washington stands in a pristine uniform, with an air of relaxed but steady determination. His hand rests on one of the cannons he captured from the British. Behind him, the sky is darkened with the dense smoke of gunfire, and shiny bayonets are grim reminders of the fierce fighting. The victorious flag of the thirteen American colonies is raised high, and the flag of the defeated British lies at Washington's feet. All these details help convey Washington's heroism and authority.

LOOK CLOSER . . .

Which of the two men looks more commanding and confident? Was your decision based on the way the leader looks and stands, or did the background setting influence what you thought?

In the background, American soldiers lead away some of the English troops they have captured. The trees are bare, because the battle took place in the freezing winter.

▲ **Charles Willson Peale**
George Washington at Princeton, c.1783
Oil on canvas
93.5 x 58.5 in.
Pennsylvania Academy of Fine Arts, Philadelphia, P.A., U.S.A.

▾ Jacques-Louis David
Napoleon in his Study, 1812
Oil on canvas
80 x 49 in.
National Gallery of Art,
Washington D.C., U.S.A.

The letters on the rolled scroll spell out part of the word "code," to show what Napoleon was writing.

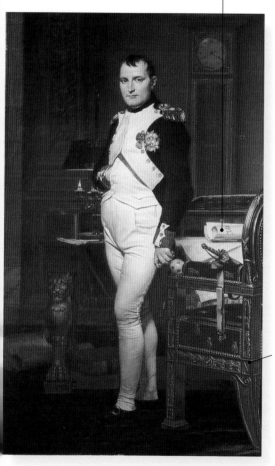

Napoleon was the emperor of France when David painted his life-sized portrait. David wanted to suggest that Napoleon was not only a heroic soldier, but also an important state leader. Napoleon stands in a grand study, wearing military uniform, decorated with medals and a general's gold epaulets on the shoulders. However, he does not look as stylish as a general should. He has unbuckled his sword and unbuttoned his cuffs. His stockings are wrinkled, and he looks distinctly unshaven. The clues in the background explain why this might be. The time on the clock reads 4:13 and the candles are burnt right down. A scroll is rolled up on the desk and a quill pen teeters on its edge, suggesting Napoleon has just put it down. These clues suggest that Napoleon has been up all night, busy working on the Napoleonic code—a set of regulations that became the basis for French law.

The emperor's chair, with its high velvet seat, resembles a throne. Napoleon's initial is included on the elaborately gilded frame.

All Together Now

In a group portrait, artists can show the relationships between people. They can make it clear how important one individual is compared with another by their size and position in the picture, and by using colors that make one particular person stand out. They can also indicate how fond people are of one another, both by how near or far away they pose together, and by the direction of their face and eyes— either toward or away from each other.

A Royal Household

At first glance, this group portrait seems to center on the five-year-old Infanta Margarita, daughter of King Philip IV of Spain. One of her maids of honor offers her a drink. Another hovers behind her. A dwarf and the court jester stand to the side, perhaps waiting to amuse the Infanta. But look again. Velázquez, the painter, has included himself in the picture, dressed as a courtier. Brush and paint palette in hand, he stares out from behind a huge canvas. What is he painting? It is impossible to know, because we can only see the back of the canvas. Some experts think he is painting a portrait of the king and queen, whose reflections can be seen in the mirror on the back wall. This means they must have been standing in the same place as us, the viewers of *Las Meninas*. So perhaps the Infanta and her retinue are gazing not at us, but at the unseene king and queen?

Velázquez managed to make the Infanta look proud and noble, even though she is so young. She later became the Empress of Austria.

SPOTLIGHT

Velázquez, like many other artists, painted on canvas, a heavy brown cloth, made from hemp or jute. He pinned it taut onto a sturdy wooden frame, known as a stretcher. Before he started painting, he coated the canvas with a layer of non-absorbent primer, so that the oil paints did not seep into the canvas. He set out and mixed his oil paints on a wooden palette and propped the canvas against a wooden easel.

Velázquez used unusually long brushes, so he could stand at a distance from his work and see the effect of his brushstrokes.

LOOK CLOSER . . .

Velázquez has made this picture a bit like a snapshot. Each person is frozen in mid-action—the jester kicks the sleeping dog, the artist steps back from his painting, a man turns on the stairs. Compare this informal grouping with the far more formal royal family overleaf.

Even though the images of the king and queen are blurred in the mirror, their faces are recognizable.

‹ Diego Velázquez
Las Meninas (The Maids of Honor)
1656
Oil on canvas
125 x 109 in.
Prado Museum, Madrid, Spain

The King and His Family

Look how carefully the members of this Spanish royal family have been posed for their formal family portrait. The king and queen take center stage. The king's many medals glisten. The queen's gold and silver dress shimmers. Ferdinand, heir to the throne, stands proudly nearest the front. The other, less important members of the family crowd around on either side. The men wear similar, splendid costumes with sashes and medals. The women wear virtually identical white, glistening dresses. Although Goya shows the family dressed magnificently, he does not flatter their looks and shows their various characters quite plainly.

ACTIVITY

Draw a group portrait of your own family. Plan it carefully, just as Goya did. Decide where to position each person. Who will be in the center or nearest the front? Who will you put side by side? Will everyone look out or will some people look toward one another?

Goya has included himself in the picture. He stands in the shadows behind the royal family in front of a large canvas. Find out more about Goya in the Timeline Album, which is included in your pack.

LOOK CLOSER . . .

Goya has made this family seem so formal by showing them all in stiff, uncomfortable poses. Their gazes go in all sorts of directions. See which ones are looking toward you and which are looking elsewhere.

▸ **Francisco de Goya**
The Family of Charles IV, 1800
Oil on canvas
110 x 132 in.
Prado Museum, Madrid, Spain

This woman with her face turned away is not a real person. Goya included her to represent the future wife of Prince Ferdinand, as yet unknown.

SPOTLIGHT

Goya used loose, visible brushstrokes to paint the glittering details in this picture. Notice how he used dabs and dots of white and yellow to conjure the effect of the shiny silver medals and the sparkling dresses and jewelry. The faces, by comparison, have been painted much more smoothly.

Happy Children?

Dressed in their best, these four children of a wealthy London doctor look carefree and cheerful as they listen to the organ that the boy is playing. But there is more to this portrait than meets the eye.

This baby is a boy called Thomas. He died before this picture was finished. Two hundred and fifty years ago, when this picture was painted, many children died very young.

Hogarth has included extra details to make us think about how short a time childhood lasts and how uncertain life can be. The fresh flowers in the girls' hair, the ripe cherries held by the oldest girl, and the bowl of luscious fruits are signs of life and growth. But notice how the cat is eyeing the caged bird, claws at the ready, waiting for an opportunity to pounce and seize it. The clock in the background signifies the passing of time. The winged boy on top of the clock holds up the scythe of Father Time, a grim reminder of death.

The glistening bowl is full of plump, fresh fruit—apples, pears, grapes, and cherries.

LOOK CLOSER . . .

Children's best clothes were simply smaller versions of adult fashions. The boy wears a frilly shirt, long waistcoat, and a satin suit. The baby boy wears a dress, which was the custom for all babies, both girls and boys.

The bird has spotted the wide-eyed cat. It anxiously flaps its wings and chirps loudly.

◀ **William Hogarth**
The Graham Children, 1742
Oil on canvas, 63 x 71 in.
National Gallery, London, U.K.

SPOTLIGHT

Notice how Hogarth uses light and shade. The four children stand out strongly against the dark room behind them, where the pictures and the pieces of furniture are murky and vague. Every detail of their smiling faces and clothes can be clearly seen. In the light, the children's skin looks pale and creamy, and their shiny satin and lacy clothes catch reflections.

A Group Portrait

SPOTLIGHT

Rembrandt was one of the first artists to use strong contrasts of light and shade (known as *chiaroscuro*) in his paintings. This technique could be used either to intensify the drama of a particular scene, or to highlight particular people, who stood out from others in the shadows.

Groups of important men in Holland often commissioned portraits of themselves. These pictures were very formal, with men lined up stiffly in rows or sitting around a table. Rembrandt, who painted this gigantic portrait of a company of soldiers, was the first to portray a group more naturally. The captain gives orders to his lieutenant, while the rest of the company prepares to march out. Rembrandt set the scene in the daytime. By a century later, the picture varnish had darkened so much that the scene seemed to be set at night, so the painting was nicknamed *The Night Watch*.

▸ **Rembrandt van Rijn**
The Military Company of Captain Frans Banning Cocq ("The Night Watch"), 1642
Oil on canvas
141 x 172 in.
Rijksmuseum, Amsterdam, Holland

Self-Portraits

Since the 15th century, many artists have painted pictures of themselves, known as self-portraits. Some were obsessed with their own appearance, others wanted to show off their painterly skills and style, and some wanted to give a message about the role of painters and painting in society. Sometimes artists painted themselves in their studios at work. Others painted themselves in the clothes of successful gentlemen. Two artists who painted themselves more often than any others were Rembrandt and van Gogh.

Young and Old

Rembrandt painted his self-portrait at every step of his career, from youth to old age. He also drew and etched his likeness over and over again, using himself as a model to experiment with the effects of light and different facial expressions. Rembrandt enjoyed dressing up. He kept exotic costumes and props in his studio, and used them for some of his self-portraits.

‹ Rembrandt van Rijn
Self-portrait as a Young Man, 1634
Oil on wood
25 x 21 in.
Uffizi Gallery, Florence, Italy

› Rembrandt van Rijn
Self-portrait, c.1665
Oil on canvas
45 x 37 in.
Iveagh Bequest, Kenwood, London, U.K.

LOOK CLOSER . . .

In addition to brushes and a paint palette, Rembrandt is holding a long *mahlstick*. Painters used one to keep their hand steady when painting fine details. Its end was padded so the stick could rest on the canvas without damaging it.

Showing Strong Emotions

Like Rembrandt, van Gogh painted a large number of self-portraits—forty-three in only four years! Sometimes he painted himself when he had no other model available, but more importantly, he tried to express in his self-portraits how he was feeling at a particular time.

Van Gogh was often deeply lonely and depressed. He had moved to the south of France, wanting to set up a colony of artists. However, the only artist he persuaded to join him was Paul Gauguin. Their differing personalities and ideas about art led to terrible arguments.

After one row, van Gogh threatened to attack Gauguin and, in a fit of madness, cut off part of his own ear. Gauguin left, and van Gogh painted this famous self-portrait, showing how sad, ill, and hopeless he felt, left by himself again.

See how van Gogh varied his brushstrokes to form textures and patterns of light and shade.

By putting dabs of red and green (two colors that "sing" together) next to one another in his eye, he has made his gaze seem very penetrating. Notice how much green there is on the rest of his face. It helps convey his feeling of illness.

LOOK CLOSER . . .

Van Gogh thought that particular colors provoked specific feelings. Yellow, the color of the warm sun, was for him an emblem of happiness. By contrast, the black fur framing van Gogh's wan face and the large, dark expanse of his blue-green jacket help suggest the gloomy atmosphere of this picture.

▲ Vincent van Gogh
Self-portrait with a Bandaged Ear, 1889
Oil on canvas, 24 x 19 in., Courtauld Institute, London, U.K.

ACTIVITY

Create your own self-portrait using colors to show your mood, rather than using them realistically. Consider what sort of expression to give yourself and whether you will stare out or have your face turned to one side.

Van Gogh admired Japanese prints. Their strong outlines and bold, bright, contrasting colors influenced the way he painted. He said, "One cannot study Japanese art, it seems to me, without becoming happier and merrier."

SPOTLIGHT

Van Gogh painted his pictures quickly and energetically. He often used paint straight from the tube, without mixing the colors. He painted with thick, raised brushstrokes (known as *impasto*). He used a variety of marks—long streaks and short dabs, both straight and wavy. See if you can find examples of all these in this picture.

Telling a Story

Some paintings tell stories, inspired either by events in the Bible, the lives of saints, or ancient myths. Early wall paintings in churches often depict the key events of a story in a series of separate pictures, rather like a cartoon strip. Other paintings show several scenes from a story in the same picture, with the main characters appearing several times. Many artists only painted the most dramatic event in a story. They included details to suggest what had happened just before. People at the time knew the stories well and recognized these details.

Heroes and Monsters

According to legend, a gruesome dragon once terrorized a city kingdom. Every day, to keep it at bay, the citizens gave it sheep to eat. When their supply of sheep ran low, the king decreed that the dragon should be given human victims instead. Lots were drawn to decide who would be sacrificed. Finally, the lot fell on the king's daughter, Cleodolinda, who was taken to the dragon's cave and left to her fate.

As she cried in despair, George, a Christian knight, happened to pass by and promised "in the name of Christ" to help her. Raphael depicted the moment when Saint George was about to slay the dragon with his sword.

Raphael imagined the dragon to be a muscly, winged monster, with powerful clawed limbs and a long tail—an inventive mixture of mammal, reptile, and bird.

LOOK CLOSER . . .

Raphael uses specific colors to emphasize the meaning of this story—the triumph of good over evil. The dragon is dark and shadowy, symbolic of the forces of evil. By contrast, Saint George wears gleaming glinting armor, and rides a white horse, a color traditionally associated with goodness and light. The princess wears red, representing the blood of the sacrificial victim.

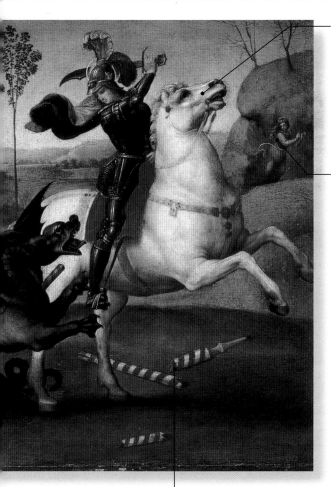

The rearing horse looks terrified. Its wild expression contrasts with the calm and determined face of Saint George, heightening the knight's bravery.

The princess looks anxiously towards Saint George, poised to run away.

The broken pieces of lance lying on the ground suggest Saint George has had a bitter struggle with the dragon. One piece has pierced the dragon's chest.

▲ **Raphael (Raffaello Sanzio)**
Saint George Fighting the Dragon, c.1505
Oil on panel
11 x 8.5 in.
Louvre Museum, Paris, France

ACTIVITY

Draw your idea of what a dragon might look like, using the features of different sorts of animals —perhaps the beak of a vulture, the wings of a bat, the claws of a tiger, the teeth of a piranha, and the tail of a crocodile.

SPOTLIGHT

Diagonal lines in paintings give a feeling of movement. Vertical lines give a sense of stillness. Raphael has created a sense of dramatic action in this picture with the lunging dragon, the rearing horse, and Saint George's raised arm.

37

Greek and Roman Myths

Can you believe that this battle is taking place at a wedding banquet? All the guests seem to have fled, but the clues are the crumpled white tablecloth and the pile of silver plates and pitchers being pulled to the ground. The painting was inspired by a Greek myth about the hero, Perseus. He had rescued the princess Andromeda from being eaten by a repulsive sea monster, and was allowed to marry her as a reward. However, Andromeda had long been promised to another man, named Phineas, who stormed into the feast to claim her for himself.

The artist depicts the moment when, heavily outnumbered by Phineas' men, Perseus holds up the snake-haired head of the frightful monster, Medusa. The eyes of Medusa turned anyone who looked at her to stone. In this picture, Phineas is in the process of turning to stone, and some of his soldiers have already become stone statues.

Minerva was the Roman goddess of defensive war. She is said to have sprung, fully grown and dressed in armor, from the mind of her father, the god Jupiter.

▲ **Jean-Marc Nattier**
Perseus Turning Phineas into Stone, 1718
Oil on canvas
447 x 575 in.
Musée de Beaux-Arts, Tours, France

LOOK CLOSER . . .

Nattier draws attention to important details in the story with highlights. The broad, bright slash of the tablecloth reminds us that the wedding feast is in ruins. The flashing glints of armor show which soldiers are still alive and moving, whereas the soldiers who have been turned to stone disappear into the shadows.

Phineas' head and arms are cool gray, whereas his legs are still fleshy brown. It's as if we are actually witnessing Phineas' transformation into stone.

Medusa's head was covered with a mass of writhing, hissing snakes. They never slept, and spat poison at anyone who approached them.

SPOTLIGHT

The arm gestures of Minerva, Perseus, and Phineas follow a diagonal line to show the sequence of action in the story. Minerva points down to Perseus to encourage him to use Medusa as a weapon to defend himself against Phineas. Perseus holds Medusa's head down toward Phineas, who recoils from it in alarm, with his left arm leaning backward.

Art for Sale!

About four hundred years ago, after a long war against Spain, Holland became an independent country. Local artists started painting pictures with which newly-wealthy townspeople decorated their homes. These paintings celebrated the beauty of the countryside they had fought so hard to win, the power of the Dutch navy, and the settled nature of people's everyday lives. Painters specialized in one type of painting—such as landscapes, townscapes, seascapes, interiors, <u>still-lifes</u>, or scenes of people at work or play.

Flower Pictures

Every flower and fruit in this wonderful arrangment has been painted with great skill to make it seem as lifelike as possible. But look closely and you'll soon discover that a display like this could never exist in real life. Why not? Because it includes flowers and fruit that never all appear at the same time. There are springtime pussy willows and fruit blossom, summery roses, carnations, and marigolds, an autumn harvest of ripe wheat and blackberries, and winter holly berries.

In addition to providing a decoration for the dining-room wall of a wealthy merchant, this picture gives a message. It reminds people that however exquisite anything in nature might be, its beauty does not last forever. Eventually, everything fades and dies. Notice, for example, how the upper flowers stand tall and upright in the light, whereas the lower ones have already begun to wilt.

▶ **Jan Davidsz de Heem**
Still Life of Flowers,
C.1670
Oil on canvas
28 x 19 in.
Johnny van Haeften Gallery,
London, U.K.

LOOK CLOSER . . .
See how many insects you can find in this picture. You should be able to spot a bee, two centipedes, a beetle, several butterflies and moths, a dragonfly, and a grasshopper—not to mention a hungry salamander.

The artist has shown on a single twig how flowers change with the passing of time. Buds form, they begin to open; petals appear and then begin to droop.

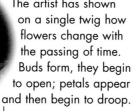

SPOTLIGHT

Flower painters waited until a particular flower or fruit was in season to paint it from life. Their paintings sometimes took as long as two years to complete. Painters probably worked on more than one painting at a time. Having planned an arrangement, they painted each flower or fruit in its space, as it appeared.

Nearly four hundred years ago, in Holland, there was a huge craze for tulips. People bought and sold rare varieties of tulip bulbs at ridiculous prices. It's hard to believe, but tulips were so valuable that it was far cheaper to buy a painting than the tulips themselves!

The artist has included glistening drops of water on some of the flowerheads to make them look fresh and real.

All Quiet in the Country

This picture welcomes us into the calm, flat, carefully cultivated Dutch countryside, where people dotted here and there are quietly busy. The two rows of tall trees, which appear to get steadily smaller, pull our eyes along the rutted road to the low horizon. Here, the vast expanse of cloudy sky meets the clustered roofs of Middelharnis, the village in the distance. A hunter strolls along the road toward us, a gun slung over his shoulder and an eager dog at his feet.

▸ **Meindert Hobbema**
The Avenue, Middelharnis,
1689
Oil on canvas, 41 x 35.5in.
National Gallery, London, U.K.

A couple has stopped to gossip in the side lane outside a farm. They help give a sense of scale in the painting.

SPOTLIGHT

Hobbema uses several <u>perspective</u> devices to give this picture a feeling of space. Trace the sides of the road and the treetops with your fingers and thumbs. Notice how the lines all meet up at a point (known as the <u>vanishing point</u>) on the horizon. Your eye is led by these lines to the vanishing point, as if you were looking into the far distance. Copy this picture, and see how the grid in your pack helps you draw the scene in proportion.

The church tower stands out against the sky, clearly visible even from far away. It reinforces how very flat the land around it is.

Have you ever seen such a grand breakfast table? Still-life pictures like this reflected the sumptuous lifestyle of successful businessmen, who could afford elegant silver tableware, delicate Chinese porcelain, fragile Venetian glasses, and expensive imported foods, such as salt, lemons, and olives.

Through careful arrangement and choice of objects, the artist could also show off his skill in painting textures and light effects. You can almost feel the roughness of the lemon peel, the smooth shell of the crab, the crusty bread, and the soft tablecloth. The sparkling glasses and the gleam of the shiny tableware dazzle the eye.

Both salt and the carefully crafted salt cellar were costly luxuries that only the wealthy could afford.

LOOK CLOSER . . .

If you could touch the objects in this painting, what different textures could you feel? What would feel knobbly, grainy, sharp, or smooth? What would feel warm or cold, hard or soft?

▾ **Willem Claez Heda**
Breakfast with Crab, 1648
Oil on canvas, 46 x 46 in.
The Hermitage, St Petersburg, Russia

For the Record

Painters sometimes recorded particular events. Rulers wanted impressive pictures of military victories, showing off their power and might, to decorate their palaces. Rich patrons wanted pictures of a specific event or a place they had visited or especially liked. Artists used their skills and imagination to create pictures that satisfied their patrons, but which were also powerful, interesting, and exciting in themselves.

Winner Takes All

Trumpets blare! Horses rear! Three knights attack the lone remaining enemy soldier as the victorious army presses forward behind its finely dressed leader. Broken lances and pieces of armor litter the ground, but only one enemy soldier lies dead. This bloodless decorative scene, set amidst exotic fruit trees and flowers, looks more like a carefully staged tournament than a real battle. It was one of three huge pictures, all similar in shape and size, that Uccello painted to decorate a room in the Medici Palace, home to the most wealthy and powerful family in Florence, Italy. They celebrated the victory of Florentine troops over their enemies from the nearby city of Siena, and displayed Uccello's obsession with _perspective_. This is a technique to make the flat surface of a picture look as if it has depth and distance.

LOOK CLOSER . . .

This painting originally hung with its bottom edge 6 feet from the floor. Hold the book at arm's length above your head and follow the lines of the slanting, broken lances with your eyes. See how they meet on Niccolò's thrusting right hand.

Niccolò da Tolentino, the Florentine leader, would not have worn a fancy hat like this for fighting, but it makes him stand out as a hero.

▾ Paolo Uccello
The Battle of San Romano,
C.1450
Tempera on wood
72 x 126 in.
National Gallery, London, U.K.

Uccello has made the back and head of the dead soldier shorter than his legs, to make them seem farther away. This is called _foreshortening_.

The decorations on the horses' harnesses were made of real gold. The knights' armor was originally made of shiny silver-leaf, but this has now tarnished.

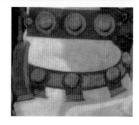

45

Shark Attack!

Help! Can the rescuers save this boy from the vicious shark? This eye-catching picture was inspired by a true event. Early one morning in 1749, Brooke Watson, a young sailor, was swimming alone in a harbor in Cuba. When a shark attacked him, his shipmates quickly rowed to the rescue.

The shark attacked twice—first tearing the flesh off Watson's right leg and then biting off his foot. Copley, the artist, deliberately chose to paint the most nail-biting moment of the story, as the shark comes back to attack for a third time. It's impossible to tell whether the young swimmer will be saved or eaten alive.

Luckily, Watson was saved. He became Lord Mayor of London and a member of Parliament. Once rich and successful, he asked Copley to paint this record of his story, almost thirty years after it happened.

LOOK CLOSER . . .

The artist has carefully positioned the swimmer and the shark for greatest effect. The picture stops at Watson's right ankle, to remind us of his cut-off foot. The shark's size is suggested by showing only its head and tail. You can only imagine the hugeness of its thrashing body beneath the waves.

SPOTLIGHT

The artist has found all sorts of ways to suggest movement. The rescue boat makes the waves frothy and choppy, as it comes alongside the helpless swimmer. The two rescuers strain forward, trying desperately to reach him. The man with hair flying pushes down on the prow, ready to thrust his boathook into the shark. Another man has thrown a rope into the water, hoping Watson will manage to grab it.

The weak swimmer seems frozen with shock. His eyes stare into the far distance, not at his rescuers.

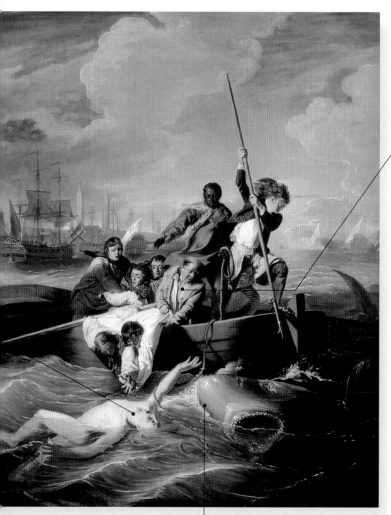

The bosun tugs on the shirt of one of the rescuers to prevent him from falling overboard.

ACTIVITY

Copley copied the sailors' frowns and grimaces from a book of facial expressions by a French artist, named le Brun. Can you draw people with expressions of surprise, worry, concentration, and shock? Think about whether their eyes should look up or down, and whether their mouths should be wide open or grimly closed.

▲ John Singleton Copley
Watson and the Shark, 1782
Oil on canvas
72 x 90.5 in.
Detroit Institute of Art, M.I., U.S.A.

Copley has given the shark imaginary lips and teeth, quite unlike the mouth of a real shark. It is unlikely that he had ever seen a real one.

Better Than a Picture Postcard

More than two hundred and fifty years ago, it was fashionable for rich, young British noblemen to go on a Grand Tour of Europe, especially Italy. These wealthy tourists bought pictures by local artists to take home as a reminder of the sights they had seen. Canaletto was one of Italy's most popular artists. He specialized in views of the celebrated sights and spectacular festivals of his native city, Venice. This picture celebrates a day of boat races, known as a "regatta."

Venice is a unique city. Instead of streets, it has a network of canals running through it. This wide Grand Canal is its Main Street. It is lined on both sides with elegant palaces and other impressive buildings. However, the view Canaletto shows of the Grand Canal is not absolutely exact. He made pencil sketches from several different viewpoints and joined them together to make a more interesting view, or "vista."

The regatta may have been part of the carnival festivities, when people wore costumes like these.

Canaletto painted buildings in very precise and realistic detail. Because the regatta was a special occasion, colorful cloths were hung over the balconies of the houses.

Canaletto brilliantly captured the unique and ever-changing quality of light in Venice.

 SPOTLIGHT

Canaletto was renowned for the way he showed patterns of light and shadow in his pictures. Notice the difference in color between the buildings bathed in sunshine compared to those in the shade, and the sharp-edged shadows.

◀ **Canaletto**
A Regatta on the Grand Canal, c.1740
Oil on canvas
48 x 72 in.
National Gallery,
London, U.K.

Venice's sleek black boats are known as gondolas. The oarsmen stand up to propel the gondolas along with a single oar.

Back to Nature

When artists paint outdoor views, they make careful choices about what landscape to show and how to show it. Some have recorded actual places, whilst others have invented imaginary landscapes. Some have included realistic details, others have distorted colors and shapes, as a way of expressing a particular emotion. Some have emphasized the lushness or peace of nature, whereas others have depicted violent storms or volcanoes. Until about two hundred years ago, artists painted finished landscape pictures in their studios—although they often made sketches outdoors beforehand.

Painting the Seasons

Brrrr, what a bitterly cold picture! Don't you feel sorry for these three hunched hunters, who trudge exhaustedly home through ankle-deep snow, with only a single fox to show for their day's hunting? Their thin dogs look equally worn out. This is one of a set of six pictures that Bruegel painted for a rich Antwerp merchant. Each one showed a slice of country life during a different season. This scene depicts both the hardships and pleasures of the freezing winter for peasant farmers.

These people are roasting a pig. The yellow and orange flames of their fire are the only warm colors in an otherwise bleak, gray landscape.

SPOTLIGHT

Although the landscape may look realistic, it is imaginary. Bruegel has combined the flat landscape of his native Holland with the high, jagged peaks of the Alps, which he had seen on his travels.

With the ground covered by deep snow, the villagers could not do any farm work. They had time to enjoy skating, sliding, sleding, and playing games on the ice.

Notice how the line of dark, bare trees leads your eye from the hilltop toward the immense, snowy panorama below. The silhouette of the swooping bird helps emphasize the impression of a wide, open sky.

One villager carries a huge bundle of firewood home. In Bruegel's time, this was the only fuel available for both heating and cooking.

◄ **Pieter Bruegel**
Hunters in the Snow, 1565
Oil on panel
46 x 64 in.
Kunsthistorisches
Museum, Vienna,
Austria

A True View?

Imagine you are standing on the bank beside the inquisitive dog, gazing at this tranquil summer scene. Admire the variety of different greens you can see. On your left is the cottage of Willy Lott, an old, deaf farmer, whom Constable had known all his life. In front of you, a cart (haywain) trundles slowly through the shallow water on its way to collect hay from the fields in the far distance. The horses enjoy the cool water on their legs. The man in the black hat waves to you as the cart passes. On the far bank, you spy a fisherman, half-hidden in the undergrowth. Painted at a time when people preferred pictures of dramatic scenes from the Bible or ancient history, Constable's tranquil landscape pictures were not very popular. However, today he is considered one of England's best landscape artists.

A woman kneels outside the cottage, dipping her hand in the water. It is not clear whether she is washing clothes or filling a bucket.

▲ **John Constable**
The Haywain, 1821
Oil on canvas
51 x 73 in.
National Gallery, London, U.K.

LOOK CLOSER . . .

Notice how small splashes of red stand out from the overall greenness of this picture. The red harnesses of the horses lead your eye toward the hay cart, the focus of the painting. The fisherman on the far bank has on a red vest.

Cloudy skies form an important part of Constable's pictures. He made hundreds of sketches of them. He thought that "no two days are alike nor even two hours," and particularly wanted to capture the changing movements and shapes of scudding clouds.

Constable used blobs and flecks of white or yellow to show bright patches of sunlight. This technique was unusual. Other painters at the time were using very smooth, blended brushstrokes. His critics called the speckles "Constable's snow."

The tiny white figures dotted across the background are haymakers, either cutting hay with their scythes or loading hay on to a cart.

SPOTLIGHT

Constable loved the countryside and wanted to paint it as directly and precisely as he could. He drew separate small <u>studies</u> of trees, skies, and views in the open air, and used them to compose his paintings, which were done afterward in his studio. Constable wrote, "the sound of water escaping from mill dams, willows, old rotten planks, slimy posts and brick-work—I love such things." Many of these elements are included in *The Haywain*.

Sensing the Mood

Would you like to have been on a ship out at sea in this storm? Turner claimed that he had been! He wrote that sailors had tied him to the mast of this steamship, so he could experience the icy blast of the wind and the force of the raging waves first hand. Although his claim is probably not true, his dramatic picture gives a vivid impression of how overwhelming such an experience might be. The dark outline of the steamship looks forlorn and fragile in the midst of such a tempestuous sea. It's hard to make out where the raging waves end and the wild sky begins.

Turner was not interested in showing the ship in detail, but it is just possible to make out the shape of its paddle wheel.

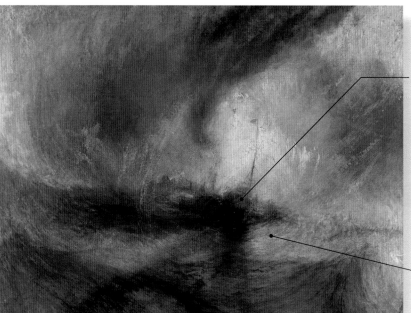

Thick brushstrokes of paint imitate the foaming waves.

▲ **Joseph Mallord William Turner**
Snowstorm: Steam-boat Off a Harbor's Mouth,
1842
Oil on canvas, 36 x 48 in., Tate Gallery, London, U.K.

LOOK CLOSER . . .

Follow the shape of the huge swirl of wind and waves. Notice how it draws your eyes into the picture toward the steamship, the central focus of the composition.

◀ **Albert
Bierstadt**
*A Storm in
the Rocky
Mountains—
Mount
Rosalie,*1866
Oil on canvas
83 x 142 in.
Brooklyn
Museum of Art,
New York,
N.Y., U.S.A.

Bierstadt painted this spectacular view of the mountains in California at a time when very few people lived in the far West. To east-coast city-dwellers, the West was considered remote, wild, and dangerous. There was no railroad and few people made the long, harsh journey there by wagon train or stagecoach.

Bierstadt's colossal, detailed landscapes gave people their first chance to see what the wilderness of America was like. They were awed and thrilled by its grandeur and beauty. Paintings like this made Americans realize the importance of protecting their country's magnificent wonders and helped inspire the creation of national parks.

Bierstadt included people in the picture to emphasize the enormous scale of the mountains.

SPOTLIGHT

People react to dark and light colors in painting, the same way they do in real life. Turner and Bierstadt chose specific colors to express moods in their paintings. Turner's limited choice of dark, somber browns, grays, and greens help conjure up the wild and angry mood of the storm. Bierstadt dramatically contrasts the dark storm clouds over the jagged peaks with the peaceful, sunlit valley.

Painting Outdoors

The people who first saw Monet's paintings thought they were unfinished. But Monet was not interested in painting views in exact detail. He was far more interested in capturing the ever-changing effects of light on a scene, at different times of day, and in all sorts of weather. Working in the open air, he painted quickly, using lively dabs, flicks, and dashes of contrasting colors. He was trying to show what he saw and felt at one particular moment. This style of painting was known as *Impressionism*. Monet was particularly fascinated by the reflections of light on water. He constructed a lily pond, spanned by a curved Japanese footbridge, in the garden of his house at Giverny, near Paris. He never tired of painting it over and over again, saying, "the effect varies constantly, not only from one season to the next, but from one minute to the next."

▾ **Claude Monet**
The Water-Lily Pond, 1899
Oil on canvas, 35 x 37 in.
National Gallery, London, U.K.

LOOK CLOSER . . .

Compare the vertical and horizontal brushstrokes and their varying colors. The darker, vertical marks help suggest the shadowy depths of the water, while the paler, horizontal ones indicate either leaves floating on the surface of the water or the reflections of afternoon sunlight.

Notice how Monet has gradually changed the size of the brushstrokes to suggest distance.

The marks at the bottom edge of the picture (the foreground) are far longer and wider than those higher up the canvas, under and beyond the bridge (the background).

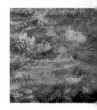

Cézanne, like Monet, painted landscapes outdoors, depicting the same view over and over again, also trying to show what he saw and felt. This is a view near Aix-en-Provence, a town in the south of France where Cézanne lived for most of his life. Unlike Monet, Cézanne worked very slowly and deliberately. He wanted to make his landscapes feel immensely solid and dense. Look how he has simplified the trees, fields and mountain, and used subtle changes of color to model their forms. Every brushstroke was important. He carefully overlapped different tones of ochre or green to create this patchwork of sun-drenched land, and used a series of different pinks and grays to depict the rough and rocky structure of the distant mountain.

SPOTLIGHT

Hold the book at arm's length. Look at the two pictures through half-closed eyes and compare how the artists have used color to create patches of light and shade. Both artists used bright colors, but Monet has used a pattern of brushstrokes, whereas Cézanne has used more regular, alternating patches of color.

▾ **Paul Cézanne**
Mont St. Victoire, 1885–7
Oil on canvas, 26 x 35 in.
Courtauld Institute, London, U.K.

A medley of brushstrokes of different greens— some grayish-green, some pale, some dark, and some greenish-blue—give this tree its shape.

The Mood of the Moment

Toward the end of the nineteenth century, a group of French Impressionists started painting scenes of modern life in Paris. The city had been recently rebuilt with wide, tree-lined avenues, alive with glittering shops and restaurants. Dressed in the latest fashion, people thronged to nighttime entertainments, such as ballet, opera, theater, circus, and dances. In their paintings, the Impressionists vividly captured the liveliness and bustle of ordinary Parisians at work and at play.

Everyday Life

Everyone looks contented and relaxed, enjoying their summer Sunday afternoon in the courtyard of Le Moulin de la Galette—an old mill converted into a dance hall. Open-air dances like this were held here every week, and lasted from mid-afternoon until midnight. They were very popular with the local working people of Montmartre, an area of Paris. Everyone came dressed in their best—some of the men are even wearing top hats!

Renoir came here on many Sundays to make oil sketches, from which he then worked in his studio to create this huge painting. Renoir captured a moment toward dusk, when the gas lamps have been lit, but sunlight still filters through the leaves of the trees overhead.

LOOK CLOSER . . .
Dabs of the same bright red and straw yellow are repeated in different places all over the canvas. How many of them can you spot?

▲ **Pierre-Auguste Renoir**
Le Moulin de la Galette, 1876
Oil on canvas
51.5 x 69 in.
John Hay Whitney Collection,
New York, N.Y.,
U.S.A.

ACTIVITY

This bustling painting has a simple structure that helps create a sense of space. Divide it diagonally with your hand, from the bottom left-hand corner to the top right-hand corner, into two triangles. See how large the foreground figures are in the lower triangle. In the upper triangle, the dancers are far smaller, and the blurred crowd behind them is smaller still, leading your eye across the large dance floor toward the trees in the distance.

Renoir was interested in the effects of dappled light. Notice the spotted pattern of light on this man's dark coat and hair.

These are Renoir's friends, whom he persuaded to come and pose for him. He painted their faces in greater detail than those of the people in the background, whom he did not know.

On Stage

Sssh! The ballet is about to begin. Degas has painted this picture as if we were part of the audience at the Paris Opera House, looking down at the dancers from a box or balcony high above the stage. The curtain has just risen. The lights pick out the ballerinas, who are poised to twirl toward us across the empty stage.

Nearly half of all Degas' oil paintings were of ballerinas. He admired the graceful and disciplined way they moved and stood. He painted them at lessons and rehearsals, getting ready in their dressing rooms or just waiting around backstage. When he painted dancers on stage, he was interested not just in the performers themselves, but also in the whole scene. He painted other views of dancers on stage, some as if spectators were looking up from the stalls or the orchestra pit, and some from the wings, looking straight across the stage.

Most of Degas' work was inspired by modern life in Paris. His favorite themes were ballet dancers, café life, circus performers and horse races. He also painted pictures of women at work, as well as portraits of wealthy people.

SPOTLIGHT

Degas was one of the first artists to be interested in photography, and it influenced compositions like this one. The unusual angle of the picture, the off-center figures, and the empty space in the foreground all create a sense of immediacy, just like a snapshot. In fact, Degas took considerable time and great care to construct views like this.

The dark brown and gray floor and the muted colors of the wooded backdrop contrast strongly with the ballerinas' costumes, making the ballerinas stand out.

Edgar Degas
Two Dancers on Stage, 1874,
Oil on canvas, 24 x 18 in.
Courtauld Institute, London, U.K.

The gleaming white
brushstrokes on the front
of the dancers' dresses
give the effect of a
footlight shining on them
from below.

LOOK CLOSER . . .

The picture focuses on a
single instant of the ballet. The
central dancer balances on her
pointes. However, the lean of her
body and arms suggests that, in
another moment, she will dance
into the space in the foreground.
The diagonal lines on the stage
reinforce the idea of movement,
as well as giving a sense of
perspective.

Degas has deliberately not
included the whole of the dancer's
other arm, to suggest that she
hasn't yet come into full view of
the spectators.

The Circus

Would you sit as stiffly and as upright as this audience if you were watching a circus show? Seurat purposely froze the spectators and emphasized the strong horizontal lines of their seats, to contrast them with the exciting action in the circus ring.

He carefully depicted the performers' movements in a series of sweeping shapes that form a circle. See how the curve of the yellow curtain, held by the open-mouthed clown, leads your eye to the ringmaster snaking his whip. The clown behind him waves toward the upside-down acrobat who bends backward and forward at the same time. The acrobat's hands and toes curve toward the bareback rider, whose arms and skirt curve upwards as she tries to keep her balance on the prancing horse. The open-mouthed clown's raised left hand and the upturned points of his hat complete the circle.

By changing the amounts of orange, white, and blue dots next to the yellow ones, Seurat created richer or paler shades of yellow throughout the picture. Blue dots were used for the shadows.

Seurat exhibited this picture before it was finished. He never completed it, because he died suddenly, two days after the show opened.

SPOTLIGHT

Seurat's time-consuming and scientific style of painting is known as *pointillism*. Rather than using colors already mixed, he painted tiny dots of pure color, closely packed, in particular combinations. When you stand 3 feet or so away from his paintings, the unmixed dots are too small to see individually, and the colors blend in your eye.

▸ **Georges Seurat**
The Circus, 189▮
Oil on canvas
71 x 58 in.
Musée d'Orsay, Paris, France

Most of the audience, as well as the rider and ringmaster, wear clothes with a v-shape. Experts have suggested that Seurat used this motif as a sign of happiness— just like when you throw your arms in the air in celebration or triumph!

The head of the clown jutting into the foreground helps make the composition of the picture more dynamic. Cover him with your fingers to see how empty and dull the circus ring looks without him.

LOOK CLOSER . . .

Seurat painted the performers in strong colors to make them stand out. The clown's red hat, the rider's dress and tights, and the acrobat's outfit are far brighter than the clothes of the audience.

Glossary

Altarpiece a religious painting or sculpture, placed on an altar table in a Christian church.

Composition the way in which different parts of a painting are put together to make a whole picture. In a well-composed painting, all areas of the picture work together to create an image that is pleasing to the eye.

Foreshortening the way in which an object is made to look shorter and narrower. Foreshortening an object can make it seem either further away or closer than it really is.

Fresco from the Italian word for "fresh." Fresco is a type of wall painting in which powdered colors are mixed with water, and painted onto damp plaster. As the lime in the plaster dries, and the water in the paint evaporates (disappears), a hard surface forms on the wall. The colors of the paint are held fast inside this surface.

Impasto a technique of painting in which the paint used is so thick that it either stands up from the canvas, or is marked with the strokes of the paintbrush. This type of paint is called 'impasted,' and is used on canvas or panel paintings.

Landscape a type of painting that shows natural scenery. Just as a landscape shows the natural environment, a townscape shows a town or city and a seascape shows the beach or sea.

Oil Paint a type of paint that is made by mixing crushed pigments with slow-drying oils, such as linseed or walnut. These oils draw in oxygen from the air to make a see-through, glossy skin that holds the color within it.

Patron someone who encourages artists, by supporting their work or giving them financial help.

Perspective a technique used to give a painting depth and distance. Discovered during the Renaissance by the Italian architect, Filippo Brunelleschi.

Pigment the ingredient of paint or dye that gives it its color. Pigment is made from animals, vegetables, minerals and, today, from modern chemicals.

Portrait a painting, or sketch, of one person or a group of people. A self-portrait is a painting by the artist of himself.

Scale the correct sizing of objects in proportion to their surroundings to create the illusion of space.

Still-life a painting or drawing of an object, or objects, that do not move. Still-life paintings are usually of fruit, flowers, food and household objects.

Studies drawings or paintings that are made in practice for (or use as) part of a larger painting.

Studio the room, or building, within which an artist works.

Tempera a technique of painting in which powdered color held in water is mixed with egg yolk.

Vanishing point the point on a painting's horizon at which all lines that run in the same direction appear to meet.

Viewpoint the position at which an artist paints a picture and from which it should be viewed. For instance, if a painting is painted from a low viewpoint, it is very dramatic and intense, and should be viewed from a distance.